Alicia Keys

by C.F. Earl

Superstars of Hip-Hop

Alicia Keys

Beyoncé

Black Eyed Peas

Ciara

Dr. Dre

Drake

Eminem

50 Cent

Flo Rida

Hip Hop:
A Short History

Jay-Z

Kanye West

Lil Wayne

LL Cool J

Ludacris

Mary J. Blige

Notorious B.I.G.

Rihanna

Sean "Diddy" Combs

Snoop Dogg

T.I.

T-Pain

Timbaland

Tupac

Usher

Alicia Keys

by C.F. Earl

Mason Crest

Alicia Keys

Mason Crest
370 Reed Road
Broomall, Pennsylvania 19008
www.masoncrest.com

Printed and bound in the United States of America.

First printing
9 8 7 6 5 4 3 2 1

Library of Congress Cataloging-in-Publication Data

Earl, C. F.
  Alicia Keys / by C.F. Earl.
      p. cm. – (Superstars of hip hop)
  Includes index.
  Discography: .
  ISBN 978-1-4222-2521-9 (hardcover) – ISBN 978-1-4222-2508-0 (series hardcover) – ISBN 978-1-4222-9223-5 (ebook)
  1. Keys, Alicia–Juvenile literature. 2. Singers–United States–Biography–Juvenile literature. I. Title.
  ML3930.K39E37 2012
  782.42164092–dc22
  [B]
                                    2011005424

Produced by Harding House Publishing Services, Inc.
www.hardinghousepages.com
Interior Design by MK Bassett-Harvey.
Cover design by Torque Advertising & Design.

Publisher's notes:
  • All quotations in this book come from original sources and contain the spelling and grammatical inconsisten-
    cies of the original text.
  • The Web sites mentioned in this book were active at the time of publication. The publisher is not responsible
    for Web sites that have changed their addresses or discontinued operation since the date of publication. The
    publisher will review and update the Web site addresses each time the book is reprinted.

DISCLAIMER: The following story has been thoroughly researched, and to the best of our knowledge, represents a true story. While every possible effort has been made to ensure accuracy, the publisher will not assume liability for damages caused by inaccuracies in the data, and makes no warranty on the accuracy of the information contained herein. This story has not been authorized nor endorsed by Alicia Keys.

Contents

Hip-Hop lingo

The Grammy Awards (short for Gramophone Awards)—or **Grammys**—are given out each year by the National Academy of Recording Arts and Sciences to people who have done something really big in the music industry.

Classical music came into being in Europe during the 1700s and 1800s. This was the music performed and enjoyed by educated people in Europe. Classical music is often symphonies or operas.

Performing means playing music, singing, or acting for other people.

Pop is short for "popular." Pop music is usually light and happy, with a good beat.

A **vocal coach** is a music teacher who shows singers how to improve their singing techniques, take care of and develop their voices, and get ready for performances.

A **manager** is someone who helps and guides a musician.

Chapter 1

Getting Started

Alicia Keys was on stage at the 2008 **Grammys**. A video of singer Frank Sinatra played behind her. Together, they sang the song "Learnin' the Blues." Alicia was singing a duet with one of the world's most famous singers!

This was a big night for Alicia. She won two awards for her song "No One." The song had been a hit on the radio. You could see the video on TV. Even though she was still young, Alicia already had a very successful career.

Alicia was the musician she'd always wanted to be. She was singing with one of the greatest in the world. She was at the top.

But life hadn't always been so great for Alicia Keys. She'd grown up in a tough neighborhood. Her family didn't have much money. Alicia's life started out a long way from the Grammys!

Growing Up

On January 25, 1981, Alicia was born in New York City. Alicia's full name was Alicia Augello Cook. Her mom, Terri Augello, was white. Alicia's dad, Craig Cook, was black.

Alicia and her family lived in New York City. They lived in a neighborhood called Hell's Kitchen. It wasn't such a nice place to live! Gangs fought in the street. Lots of people didn't have enough money.

Alicia used music to hide from the things going on in the streets. Her mother was always on her side. So when Alicia wanted to play Dorothy in *The Wizard of Oz*, her mom helped her try out for the part. The music teacher listened to Alicia sing. She knew right away that Alicia was a great singer.

Alicia also found out that she loved playing the piano. Her family didn't have much money, but her mom knew how important the piano was to Alicia. So Alicia's mom signed her up for piano lessons. Alicia was going to learn **classical** piano.

First Steps into Music

Alicia learned piano in the Suzuki style. The Suzuki style is based on the idea of language. Think of how you learned to speak when you were younger. Think about how hard it is for many adults to learn a new language. Suzuki-style music lessons teach children the language of music.

Suzuki music students must learn by listening, practicing, and playing music as much as they can. Students go to concerts to hear music. They listen to music at home every day.

Students also become friends with other kids who are learning about music. They get together and play in groups. Kids taking Suzuki lessons have to live with music all the time.

Suzuki students perform in public a lot, too. This keeps students from being scared to play in front of people. Students learn to enjoy **performing**.

They also help each other do better. They support each other and work together in their lessons.

Alicia was introduced to music while still a young child. She took classical piano lessons taught in the Suzuki method. Dr. Shinichi Suzuki introduced this technique as a way to teach very young children violin and piano.

Parents of Suzuki students play a big part, too. They must watch their student practice every day. They also have to come to each lesson. This way, students feel they have help learning their instrument.

All this was exciting for Alicia. She learned a lot about music in her lessons. She learned to love classical music. Alicia learned to understand music in ways that many **pop** musicians don't. She'd use those skills for the rest of her life.

Best of all, Alicia's lessons let her spend a lot of time with her mother. Alicia and her mom became even closer. Terri always made sure to give Alicia love and support.

Early Choices

When Alicia turned eleven, though, she felt like her lessons were getting to be too much for her. She had friends she wanted to see. She wanted to do the things other kids were doing. But her music lessons kept her too busy.

Alicia was working very hard on her music. Maybe even too hard.

Alicia told her mother how unhappy she felt. She said that music lessons weren't as fun as they used to be. Terri, Alicia's mom, knew that something needed to change.

The music lessons were good for Alicia, but they were hard, too. Terri spoke with Alicia's piano teacher. They talked it over. Then they decided that Alicia should keep going to piano lessons.

Terri told Alicia, "You can quit anything else, but you can never give up your piano lessons."

Terri's decision was a hard one to make. She knew that Alicia needed to stick with her piano. This meant Alicia would have to give up other things. But Alicia knew sticking with music was the right thing to do!

Hip-Hop Meets Classical

Alicia loved classical piano, but she liked other types of music, too. Alicia listened to pop music and hip-hop.

Hip-hop music had been around for about ten years when Alicia was born. The music started in the Bronx, an area in New York City. At the time, many people living in the city couldn't find work. Times were tough, and many families were poor.

Through music, young people could talk about their lives. You didn't need to have any money to rhyme. You never had to pay for a beat or rhythm. Making hip-hop music with friends didn't cost anything. It was a great way for young people to get together, too.

Like Alicia, many young people wanted to get out their feelings through music. Hip-hop gave them a way to do this.

Alicia learned to love both piano and hip-hop. Today, Alicia is known for mixing piano and hip-hop sounds. She made her own sound by putting two kinds of music together.

Alicia soon formed her own singing group with three friends. The group was called Embish'n. They practiced every day after school. The group met at the Police Athletic League on 124th Street. Alicia played piano and sang. Conrad Robinson was the group's **vocal coach**.

After a while, Embish'n got a **manager**. They wanted to look for places to play for people. But their manager thought they were just pretty girls. He didn't know that the group had real talent. He didn't know that Alicia was such a good musician, either.

Conrad Robinson knew Alicia was special, though. He saw that she was very talented, even if the manager didn't. He knew Alicia's life in music was just getting started.

Hip-Hop lingo

A **record label** is a company that produces music for singers and groups and puts out CDs.

An **album** is a group of songs collected together on a CD.

R&B stands for "rhythm and blues." It's a kind of music that African Americans made popular in the 1940s. It has a very strong beat. Today, it's a style of music that's a lot like hip-hop.

African Americans started **soul** music by combining the gospel music they sang in church with rhythm and blues. Soul music has a strong rhythm. It's the kind of music that makes you feel like clapping your hands or dancing.

Jazz is a kind of music that began in America. As they play, jazz musicians make up musical patterns around a basic tune. It has a strong rhythm that can change throughout the song.

A **contract** is a written agreement between two people. Once you've signed a contract, it's against the law to break it. When a musician signs a contract with a music company, the musician promises to give all her music to that company for them to produce as CDs and sell—and the music company promises to pay the musician a certain amount of money. Usually, a contract is for a certain period of time.

Billboard is a magazine that keeps track of which songs are most popular.

A **tour** means to travel around and play music for people at concerts.

Chapter 2

Alicia's Early Music

When Alicia was twelve, she entered the Performing Arts School. There, she learned more about music. She sang in choir and wrote songs.

At her new school, Alicia could focus on her music. Her teachers helped her become an even better singer.

At first, she copied other singers. If she liked a singer, she tried to sound like her. She used to sing like Mary J. Blige. But Alicia was really searching for her own sound. She was trying to find her own voice.

Alicia's life wasn't all about music, though. She did the things other teenagers do, too. Alicia went to school. She hung out with friends. She did her homework.

As Alicia grew up, her music got better and better. She went to school during the day and played music at night. She performed in many places around New York City. She wanted to play anywhere she could. She wanted to play for anyone who would listen.

Slowly, Alicia was becoming better known in New York. People remembered her voice and piano playing. Her school life was busy, too, though. She had to be a student AND a performer.

Alicia finished high school early. She was just sixteen when she graduated. When she left high school, she was the best student in her class. Columbia University accepted her as a student.

Much of Alicia's time as a child was spent playing the piano. Despite the hard work and discipline the lessons required she loved playing, and she was very good at it. She developed a love for the classical composers, which influences her music today.

A Tough Decision

Alicia's music was becoming more popular. Her style was new and cool. She mixed hip-hop and classical music. It was something people hadn't heard before.

Conrad Robinson was still Alicia's voice coach. He had helped her since she was in Embish'n. Conrad knew Alicia was a special singer. He spoke with his brother Jeff Robinson about Alicia. Jeff began to search for a **record label** for Alicia. He wanted to find a record label that fit her style.

Soon, Alicia signed a record deal with Columbia Records. But there were only a few days before her college classes started. She had to pick—Columbia Records or Columbia University?

Playing music and being a student at the same time was tough. Alicia was ready to work hard on both, but now she needed to make a choice. Again, she couldn't do it all. She had to decide between music and other parts of her life.

Alicia didn't want to leave college. Learning had always been important to her. But she couldn't do both school and music. She knew music was too important to her to give up. She decided music was best for her. She would go with Columbia Records.

Starting Out in the Music World

Alicia started working on new songs. She worked with many people she'd never met before. At first, she was nervous. Everything was so new. Everyone knew what to do but her.

Alicia was worried that she was too young. She thought other people didn't think she was good enough. She thought they might think she was just a kid.

Soon, Alicia learned what made her special. She had a new style and a new sound. People liked her music. They wanted to hear her.

Alicia had to learn to believe in herself. She had to believe in her own talents.

Alicia used her classical training to help her. She used all the skills she'd learned. She wanted to prove how talented she was.

She also used her life in New York City to help her. The busy streets of the city were beautiful to Alicia. New York is home to many different people. Each person's story helps to make the city special. To Alicia, New York City was all about mixing things together. Just like her music, the city had new and old parts. The city was part classical, part hip-hop. It was both beautiful and tough.

As Alicia learned more about herself, she learned more about business too. Soon, Alicia knew that Columbia Records wasn't right for her. The record company wanted to make money using Alicia's music. She just wanted to make good music.

Alicia ended up leaving Columbia Records. Alicia still had her manager, Jeff Robinson, though. She and Jeff had to look for other record labels.

Success

In 1999 Alicia was seventeen. She was playing shows, trying to get people to hear her. Soon, a man named Clive Davis noticed her.

Clive Davis was a businessman at Arista Records. He was well known for working with many famous singers. He helped people like Bruce Springsteen and Carlos Santana. Now, he wanted to help Alicia.

Clive Davis knew Alicia was a great musician. She could sing and play piano very well. She understood what made good songs, too. She knew more about music than a lot of other musicians. Clive Davis signed Alicia to his record label, Arista Records.

Besides classical music, Alicia loved much of the same music that others her age did, hip-hop and pop. Unlike most people her age, though, she was able to combine all those musical forms into something new and exciting.

Alicia thought it was time to use a new name. If she was going to be a musician, she wanted something special. She needed a name that told other people about her and her music. At first, Alicia thought she might use the last name "Wilde." But another name was a better fit.

Alicia's manager told her about a dream he had. In his dream, he needed to unlock a briefcase. Alicia had an idea for a name. What about "Keys"? What name could be better for a piano player?

Alicia Augello Cook had finally become Alicia Keys. She was on her way to being a star.

Songs in A Minor

Now, Alicia had a new name. She had Clive Davis behind her. Soon, she started work on her first **album**, *Songs in A Minor*.

Clive Davis wanted the world to hear the song "Fallin'." He knew it was a great song. He thought it could be a big hit for Alicia.

"Fallin'" is a song about love. It's a song about how being in love isn't always perfect. "Fallin'" was different than other songs at the time. It had parts that sounded like classical piano. Its beat sounded like R&B or hip-hop. Clive Davis thought it was a song that showed off Alicia's talent.

Because it was different, radio stations didn't want to play the song. They didn't understand what kind of music it was. Was it pop? **R&B**? It had parts of **soul** and **jazz**, too. Was kind of song was it?

What they didn't understand was that "Fallin'" was many things put together. Clive Davis knew the song was special. If the radio wouldn't play the song, he knew he had to find another way people could hear it.

He sent a letter to Oprah Winfrey. Clive wanted Alicia to go on Oprah's show and play "Fallin'." Oprah agreed, and Alicia went on the show.

After she played "Fallin'," more and more people wanted to buy the song. People loved her new sound and style of music. She was a great singer and a great piano player.

After *Oprah*, Alicia played at a party Clive Davis held. Jay Leno, the host of *The Tonight Show*, saw her play there. He liked her music. He asked her to come on his television show to play.

Alicia was already becoming a star!

Clive Davis is one of the biggest names in the recording industry. With his guidance, Alicia's career skyrocketed. He knew just what to do to make her a superstar, including writing a letter to media powerhouse Oprah Winfrey asking to have Alicia on her show.

Davis's hard work promoting Alicia wouldn't have been successful if she wasn't talented. And everyone agreed that she had the talent. In 2001, she won two *Billboard* Music Awards, including Female New Artist of the Year and Hip-Hop New Artist of the Year.

Clive Davis soon left Arista Records. He started his own company. Clive called it J Records. Alicia left Arista and signed a **contract** with the company.

Songs in A Minor was finally ready to sell in 2001. After all her hard work, her first album was done. It sold 235,000 copies in its first week. It was number one on the **Billboard** charts. It sold better than all the other music that came out that week.

Alicia's album kept selling more and more. Soon, it had sold more than a million copies. It showed off Alicia's talents. The album's style was all her own. It was a mix of her classical training and her love for newer kinds of music.

Alicia seemed to be everywhere now. She played more and more shows. By the end of 2001, *Rolling Stone* magazine named Alicia the Best New Artist of the Year. Alicia also started her first **tour** of the country.

The year had been a big one. Alicia Keys had finally become the musician she always wanted to be. She was ready to make more music. She wanted to play for more people. She was ready to take on the world.

Hip-Hop lingo

Rap is a kind of music where rhymes are chanted, often with music in the background.

Acoustic instruments are played without electricity.

Chapter 3

Fame and Fortune

At the beginning of 2002, Alicia was already a star. Her new song "A Woman's Worth" was a hit. Alicia was also getting ready for awards shows.

Alicia went to the American Music Awards in January. There, she won two awards. She won Favorite New Artist and Favorite Soul/R&B Artist.

In February, Alicia went to her first Grammy Awards. That night, she won five awards. She won for Best New Artist and for Song of the Year. She won other awards, too.

Alicia was just twenty-one years old, but she had already come so far. Only two other women had ever won as many Grammys in one night.

The awards didn't stop at the Grammys, either. Alicia won awards almost every month in 2002. People simply loved her music.

People kept buying *Songs in A Minor*. Alicia's music became even more popular.

An important part of Alicia's success has been the producing talents of Kerry "Krucial" Brothers. Many people wonder if their collaboration went beyond the music world.

An Important Friend

Kerry "Krucial" Brothers was always a good friend to Alicia. They had met when they were teenagers in New York City. They both loved music and got along well.

Together, Kerry and Alicia worked to find her special sound. Kerry liked **rap** and hip-hop. Alicia liked classical music, soul, and R&B. Kerry had worked with Alicia for many years before she became famous. He had helped Alicia make *Songs in A Minor*.

Mixing their two favorite kinds of music made Alicia's sound different. Alicia also liked having a friend who knew her well. Being famous made having good friends even more important to Alicia.

Kerry Brothers has been with Alicia since the beginning. They're close friends and great musical partners. He is still a big part of Alicia's success today.

The Diary of Alicia Keys

Soon, it was time for Alicia to make her next album. Alicia worked on the album in 2003.

Alicia decided that her second album would be called *The Diary of Alicia Keys*. She said, "It's kind of a journey inside, into my mind."

Alicia's second album mixed many different styles, like her first had. Alicia kept taking all the music she enjoyed and making it her own.

The album came out in December 2003. In its first week, it sold 618,000 copies. Alicia was definitely a star now. By January of 2004, the album had sold more than two million copies.

In the spring of 2004, Alicia went on tour again. This time, she toured with Beyoncé and Missy Elliot. Together, they were three of the most famous women in music. In September, Alicia went to China. There, she played a show on the Great Wall.

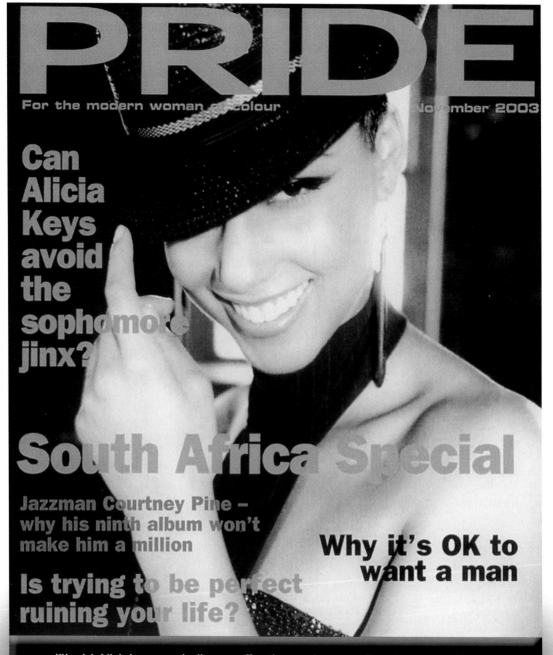

PRIDE

For the modern woman of colour   November 2003

Can Alicia Keys avoid the sophomore jinx?

South Africa Special

Jazzman Courtney Pine – why his ninth album won't make him a million

Why it's OK to want a man

Is trying to be perfect ruining your life?

Would Alicia's second album suffer the sophomore jinx that had plagued many other artists? Even the cover of the November 2003 issue of *Pride* asked that question. No one need have worried though. *The Diary of Alicia Keys* was a huge success critically and commercially.

Many songs from *The Diary of Alicia Keys* became popular. "If I Ain't Got You" was a big hit for Alicia. Alicia also did a song with singer Usher called "My Boo." The song soared to number one.

As Alicia toured, she kept winning awards. In February 2005, she went back to the Grammys. This time, she ended up with four awards. *The Diary of Alicia Keys* won Best R&B Album.

Alicia also won awards for "My Boo" and "If I Ain't Got You." She got another award for the song "You Don't Know My Name."

The Diary of Alicia Keys was another success for Alicia. She had made a second great album that fans loved!

Unplugged

After *The Diary of Alicia Keys*, Alicia wanted to try something different. In 2005, she played on the MTV show *Unplugged*.

On *Unplugged*, musicians play their songs differently, using only **acoustic** instruments. Artists play their songs more quietly and simply. They might use fewer instruments. Some artists put out an *Unplugged* album after the show, too.

For Alicia, *Unplugged* was about getting back to her roots. She wanted to make her *Unplugged* show about her and her piano. The show was all about her musical skills.

In October of 2005, Alicia's *Unplugged* album came out. It sold almost 200,000 copies in the first week.

Alicia was still going strong. Her music was popular and respected. But music wasn't all she could do. Soon, she'd share her other talents with the world.

Hip-Hop lingo

AIDS is a disease caused by the HIV virus. It is passed from one person to another by having unsafe sex or from mothers to their unborn babies. It kills millions of people every year.

Creative means using your skills or talents to make something, like music or art.

Chapter 4

Doing More

Alicia had been lucky all her life. She had great talent for music. She had love from her mother and friends. Now she had success, too.

Having success isn't much without giving something back, though. Using her success to help others is important to Alicia.

Alicia has tried to help fight **AIDS** in Africa. In 2003, she helped start the charity Keep A Child Alive. The group helps to get AIDS medicine to kids who need it.

Alicia tries to teach people about AIDS, too. She wants people to know what a big problem the disease is. She also wants people to know how they can help.

In 2005, Alicia was in an ad to teach people about AIDS. Will Smith, Tom Hanks, and other stars were in the ad, too. The ad was meant to make people think about how many people have AIDS in Africa. Did you know that 25 million people in Africa have AIDS?

Alicia also helps people in other ways. She works with a group called Frum Tha Ground Up. The group tries to help young people do their best. It helps kids to do well in school. Alicia says she wants to help kids to succeed.

Alicia has performed for charity many times, too. In 2005, she played at Live 8. Live 8 was a concert to raise money for poor people in Africa. Alicia also helped raise money for people who were in Hurricane Katrina. After the 2010 earthquakes, she played at concerts to raise money for Haiti, as well.

In 2005, Alicia met Ugandan Grace Akampumuza, a person with AIDS and a medic, as well as Michael Weinstein, president of the AIDS Healthcare Foundation at the Black Ball in New York City, part of the Global Health Summit.

In 2005, Alicia was one of the performers generously giving their time at the ReAct Now: Music & Relief concert. Held at MTV studios in New York City, the concert raised funds to aid in hurricane relief efforts along the U.S. Gulf Coast.

Alicia works with Russell Simmons, too. He runs the Hip-Hop Summit Action Network (HSAN). HSAN works to help young African American adults succeed in school. The group also encourages young people to vote for what they believe.

KrucialKeys

When Alicia was young, lots of people helped her. They gave her the chance she needed. Now, Alicia wanted to help others. She wanted others to have their own chance to make music.

Alicia isn't limiting herself to performing, or even to the music industry. She's part of the music production company, KrucialKeys, as well as of Big Pita, Lil' Pita, a television production company. She's even made her film debut. Plus, Alicia is also a best-selling author.

In 2005, Alicia and Kerry Brothers started a production company called KrucialKeys. Alicia and Kerry could now help other musicians. They would help people write songs and record music.

Alicia and Kerry also opened their own studio. They called it The Oven Studios. The Oven Studios was the new home for KrucialKeys. Alicia and Kerry could work there on music for Alicia or others.

Kerry had been with Alicia since she started. They had been friends for a long time. Alicia knew she could work well with Kerry on all sorts of music. KrucialKeys was just the next step for Kerry and Alicia.

Big Pita, Lil' Pita, and Movies

Soon, Alicia wanted to do more than music. She knew she could be **creative** in other ways. Alicia wanted to make movies and TV shows, too.

In 2006, Alicia started a company called Big Pita, Lil' Pita. Her friend and manager, Jeff Robinson, helped her start the company. Alicia said the company's first project would be a TV show. Alicia told fans the show would be about a young girl growing up in New York City.

The show would take a lot from Alicia's life. Like Alicia, the main character would be both black and white. Alicia said she didn't want her show to be like others. She wanted it to be about things other shows don't talk about.

Alicia also wanted her company's shows and movies to have strong women in them. "I was mostly raised by very strong women," said Alicia. "And I consider myself one as well."

Alicia's company next made a deal with Disney. Big Pita, Lil' Pita wanted to make movies based on older Disney movies.

Big Pita, Lil' Pita is another way for Alicia to be creative. She can show the world another side of herself through the company.

Alicia on the Silver Screen

Alicia doesn't just want to MAKE TV shows and movies. She's also in them! In 2006, she acted in her first movie. The movie was called *Smokin' Aces.* Ben Affleck and Don Cheadle also starred in it.

Alicia plays the lead in *Composition in Black and White*, a film about piano prodigy Philippa Schuyler, a child of a biracial couple who felt inter-racial marriage could help solve many social problems. Philippa was killed in 1967 during a mission to evacuate Vietnamese orphans.

In *Smokin' Aces*, Alicia plays Georgia Sykes. She is a woman paid to kill people. Alicia said that her fans under eighteen shouldn't watch the movie. This is because the movie has bad words and violence in it. *Smokin' Aces* showed a different side of Alicia. She got to be dangerous and tough.

The other actors in *Smokin' Aces* thought Alicia was a great actor. They said she was easy to work with.

Alicia was just getting started. In 2007, she co-starred in *The Nanny Diaries*. The movie was based on a book with the same name. Scarlett Johansson and Chris Evans were also in the movie.

Now, Alicia was busier than ever. She was doing lots of different things at once. Alicia's first love was still music, though. And she wasn't done making more.

Hip-Hop lingo

A **single** is one song taken from an album and sold by itself.

The **chorus** is the part of a song that repeats between verses.

A **studio album** is a collection of songs put together in a recording studio.

A **live album** is collection of songs recorded at a concert.

Tracks are parts—usually songs—of an album.

A **producer** is the person in charge of putting together songs. A producer makes the big decisions about the music.

Chapter 5

True to Herself

In 2006, Alicia and Kerry Brothers started working on Alicia's next album. Alicia said that her new album would be different from her others. She wanted to get away from the sound of her first two albums. She wanted to make an album that used even more styles of music.

This album would be called *As I Am*. It came out in November 2007. *As I Am* sold 742,000 copies in one week—faster than any of Alicia's other albums.

As I Am reached number one on the *Billboard* album charts. It sold more than any of the other albums released that week. Alicia had had all four of her albums reach number one. Britney Spears was the only other woman to have so many hit albums.

Alicia's first **single** from *As I Am* was called "No One." "No One" became a huge hit. It was one of Alicia's most popular songs.

The 2008 Grammys were big for Alicia. She won best R&B song for "No One." She also won Best Female R&B Vocal Performance for the song. Later that year, Alicia won Best Female R&B Artist at the MTV Music Awards.

The year wasn't over, though.

For the 2008 James Bond movie *Quantum of Solace*, Alicia and musician Jack White wrote and performed the theme song. Jack White was a rock musician. His style was very different from Alicia's. They worked well together, though. Their song, "Another Way to Die," was a success

Alicia also starred in the movie *The Secret Life of Bees*. The movie was based on a book by Sue Monk Kidd. Alicia won a NAACP Image Award for her acting in the movie.

Alicia was still winning awards for *As I Am* in 2009, too. At the 2009 Grammys, Alicia won Best Female R&B Vocal Performance for the song "Superwoman."

Next, Alicia worked with rapper Jay-Z on the song "Empire State of Mind." The song was for Jay-Z's album *The Blueprint 3*. "Empire State of Mind" is all about New York City, Alicia's hometown. Alicia sang the song's **chorus**. She helped write the song, too.

In 2009, *Billboard* magazine named Alicia number five in its list of top artists of the decade (2000–2009). It ranked "No One" number six in the top-100 songs of the decade.

The Element of Freedom

Alicia released her next album, *The Element of Freedom*, at the end of 2009. The album sold 417,000 in its first week.

The Element of Freedom was Alicia's fourth **studio album**. Counting *Unplugged*, her **live album**, it was her fifth. The first single from *The Element of Freedom* was called "Doesn't Mean Anything."

The album had songs with Jay-Z and Beyoncé on it, too. Jay-Z rapped on a song called "Empire State of Mind (Part II) Broken Down." The song follows "Empire State of Mind" from Jay-Z's *Blueprint 3* album. Beyoncé sang with Alicia on the song "Put It in a Love Song." Kerry "Krucial" Brothers helped with most of the songs on *The Element of Freedom*, too.

The Element of Freedom showed that Alicia was still making great music. After five albums, she wasn't going to slow down.

Marriage

Alicia met **producer** Swizz Beatz in 2009. They worked on a song together for singer Whitney Houston. In May of that year, Swizz Beatz told his fans that he and Alicia were dating.

Swizz Beatz—as you might think—is known for his beats. He produces **tracks** for a lot of different rappers. He even raps on a few songs himself. Swizz Beatz is one of the most popular hip-hop producers working today.

A year after they got together, Alicia and Swizz Beatz were engaged. They got married on July 31, 2010. They had a wedding celebration on the French island of Corsica.

A few months later, in October, Alicia gave birth to her first child, a son named Egypt. She and Swizz Beatz couldn't have been happier.

The Future

Alicia's future is bright. She's a talented and successful musician. She's an actress who has been in many movies. She's found how she can give back. Now, she's happily married and enjoying her family.

Alicia worked hard to get where she is today. She came a long way from Hell's Kitchen!

Alicia always had talent. But she also worked hard to use her talent. She stuck with her music, even when it was a hard choice to make. She kept at it, though. She kept going even when it was tough.

Alicia didn't try to sound like everyone else. She wanted to sound different. She wanted to sound like herself. When others

Alicia Keys is a gifted singer/songwriter, author, actress, and philanthropist. She's also very lucky she gets to do what she loves and, through that, give back to others in the world. She is truly making a difference.

didn't understand her music, she kept going. Alicia's style was all her own. She mixed new sounds with older sounds, hip-hop with classical. She became a success by sticking to the music she wanted to make, by being different. Today, she's known all over the world.

Where's Alicia going next? It's hard to say. Alicia's said she's working on another album and even performed a new song. Music is her first passion, but Alicia's shown that she can do so much more.

Alicia can sing, play piano, and act. She helps other musicians. She works to fight AIDS in Africa. She also helps keep kids in school in the United States. Alicia is a strong woman who can do anything she puts her mind to.

Alicia believes it's important to be true to yourself. She says you have to do what you love, no matter what. Giving back and being creative are important to Alicia. She wants to do what she loves and help others while doing it.

Whether classical or R&B, movies or music, one thing is for sure. No matter what Alicia does next, she'll always stay true to herself.

1981	Alicia Augello Cook is born on January 25 in New York City.
1999	Alicia signs with Clive Davis of Arista Records.
2001	*Songs in A Minor* is released.
	Alicia performs at fundraising benefits for victims of the September 11 terrorist attacks.
2002	"A Woman's Worth" hits Billboard's Top-10 Chart.
	Alicia wins five Grammy Awards, tying the record for most Grammys won by a female artist.
2003	*The Diary of Alicia Keys* is released.
2005	Alicia wins four Grammy Awards.
	She performs at the Live 8 concerts.
	She performs at ReAct Now: Music and Relief, a benefit to raise money for people affected by Hurricane Katrina.
	She performs at Shelter from the Storm: A Concert for the Gulf Coast to raise money for victims of Hurricane Katrina.
	Tears for Water: Songbook of Poems and Lyrics is released. It is Alicia's first book.
	Alicia Keys Unplugged is released.
2006	Alicia makes her film debut in *Smokin' Aces.*
	She tours Uganda to promote care for children affected by AIDS.
2007	Alicia appears in the film *The Nanny Diaries.*
	As I Am is released.

2008 Alicia wins two Grammys for "No One" on *As I Am*.

She appears in the film *The Secret Life of Bees*.

2009 Alicia wins one Grammy for "Superwoman" on *As I Am*.

The Element of Freedom is released.

2010 Alicia marries rapper/producer Swizz Beatz.

Alicia gives birth to her first child, son Egypt.

2011 Alicia re-releases *Songs in A Minor* for the albums tenth anniversary.

In Books

Baker, Soren. *The History of Rap and Hip Hop*. San Diego, Calif.: Lucent, 2006.

Comissiong, Solomon W. F. *How Jamal Discovered Hip-Hop Culture*. New York: Xlibris, 2008.

Cornish, Melanie. *The History of Hip Hop*. New York: Crabtree, 2009.

Czekaj, Jef. *Hip and Hop, Don't Stop!* New York: Hyperion, 2010.

Haskins, Jim. *One Nation Under a Groove: Rap Music and Its Roots*. New York: Jump at the Sun, 2000.

Hatch, Thomas. *A History of Hip-Hop: The Roots of Rap*. Portsmouth, N.H.: Red Bricklearning, 2005.

Websites

Alicia Keys Daily
www.aliciakeysdaily.com

AliciaKeysFan.com
www.aliciakeysfan.com

Alicia Keys' Official Site
www.aliciakeys.com

Alicia Keys Online Fansite
www.alicia-keys.net

Discography

Albums

2001	Songs in A Minor
2003	The Diary of Alicia Keys
2005	Unplugged
2007	As I Am
2009	The Element of Freedom

Index

Index

About the Author

C.F. Earl is a writer living and working in Binghamton, New York. Earl writes mostly on social and historical topics, including health, the military, and finances. An avid student of the world around him, and particularly fascinated with almost any current issue, C.F. Earl hopes to continue to write for books, websites, and other publications for as long as he is able.

Picture Credits

AFP Photo/Lee Celano: p. 6
Chris Alred/Keystone/Getty Images: p. 9
Dreamstime.com/Sbulkey: p. 1
Dreamstime.com/Featureflash: p. 36
Fashion Wire Daily/Maria Ramirez: p. 24
J Records/NMI: p. 17, 34, 40
Michael Loccisano/FilmMagic: p. 31
NMI/Michelle Feng: p. 26
PRNewsFoto/NMI: p. 14
PRNewsFoto/NMI: p. 30
Robyn Mackenzie: p. 12
Russ Einhorn/Star Max: p. 19
Stuart Price/AFP/Getty Images: p. 28
UPI/Roger Williams: p. 20
Zuma Press/Bavarel/MITI/Visual: p. 22
Zuma Press/NMI: p. 32

To the best knowledge of the publisher, all other images are in the public domain. If any image has been inadvertently uncredited, please notify Harding House Publishing Services, Vestal, New York 13850, so that rectification can be made for future printings.